THE ORACLE BOOK OF KNITTING

This book is dedicated to all ORACLE Knitters

Joy Gammon

THE ORACLE BOOK OF
Knitting

Weidenfeld and Nicolson   London

Published in Great Britain by
George Weidenfeld & Nicolson Limited
91 Clapham High Street
London SW4 7TA

Photoset by Deltatype, Ellesmere Port
Printed in Great Britain by The Guernsey Press Co. Ltd, Guernsey, C.I.

Contents

Acknowledgements

Particular thanks go to all the ORACLE Knitters who
contributed, joined in, or simply took an encouraging interest in
the making of this book.

I would also like to thank the Editor and staff of ORACLE
Teletext, and everyone at Spectrum Yarns for all their help, and
for the supply of all the yarns for the garments in the book. All
yarns used contain Courtelle.

The Photographs are by Glen Pearson Photography.

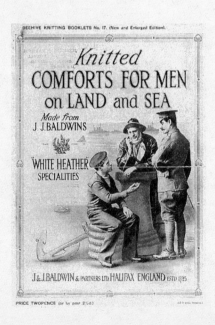

Preface

From *The Knitter's Friend*, an early book of knitting 'Receipts'

In selecting Receipts for this little Volume, the chief care has been, that while they should be useful, elegant, and clearly defined, they should be also those that have been hitherto unpublished. From the difficulty of recognition in some cases, of the same receipt differently described, it must be evident it was no easy task to avoid all those contained in the several works already published. I have endeavoured to do so, and if I have not succeeded, I crave pardon alike of my patrons and those whose property I have thus unintentionally invaded, trusting they will accept this my apology, and promising that, on receiving intimation of such trespass, the offender shall be excluded from the next impression, should I attain to it.

In conclusion, I beg to return my most sincere thanks to those Ladies and Gentlemen whose contributions have added much to the value of this volume,

> And remain,
>
> Their obliged and grateful servant,
>
> THE EDITRESS

The Knitter's Prayer

I pray when risen from the dead
I may in glory stand,
Perhaps a crown upon my head,
But needles in my hand.

I never learned to sing or play,
So let no harp be mine.
From childhood to my dying day
Plain knitting's been my line.

And so, accustomed to the end
In plying useful stitches,
I'll be content if given to knit
The little Angels' breeches.

CONTRIBUTED BY PAT CLACK

Introduction

Since November 1983 I have had the delightful job of writing the Knitting pages on ORACLE Teletext. During this time I have met many of the people who read the pages, and have received many hundreds of letters from readers, some asking questions, some offering solutions, and many simply exchanging news and ideas.

Because ORACLE is ephemeral we decided that it would be a good idea to write a book so that ORACLE knitters could have some patterns to keep, and also some of the many tips and hints that have been on teletext through the years.

I also asked, without realising what I had started, if any of you out there had any old patterns which you did not want, and which ORACLE could swap with you for new ones. This resulted in a fascinating avalanche of patterns both ancient and fairly modern, which were so interesting that I wanted a way of showing some of them to you. Many of them have now been included in the ORACLE Knitting Pattern Collection, and I take them to as many of my talks around the country as I can so that you can see them. Duplicates and recent patterns were sold for charity, but extracts from the most evocative and beautiful are used to decorate this book. One has even been turned into a modern pattern for you to try your hand at knitting.

At various times talented readers have sent in poems, prayers and limericks, and I would like to thank you for all the letters and ideas you sent in. I am delighted to be able to include some of these in this book and I hope to show on the screen all those for which there has not been room here.

Another talent of our viewers is knitting design. I decided to run a competition in which knitters were invited to design a jumper. I intended to put only the winning design in this book as a pattern, but there were so many entries and the standard was so high that the five runners-up are also patterned in the book. I am sure you will agree that they are most successful, and I would like to thank everyone who entered all the wonderful drawings, which were a difficult pleasure to sort and judge. Congratulations to everyone who was successful.

So, ORACLE Knitters, this is very much *your* book. Thank you very much for all your support and company, your ideas and suggestions, and for reading ORACLE. I hope that you enjoy the book, and have as much fun making the garments as I did.

See you on ORACLE, all best wishes,

Joy Gammon

How to use the book

There are twelve knitting patterns in the book, and at the beginning of each there is a relevant collection of hints and tips about a particular knitting technique which applies to the pattern but is also helpful with other knitting.

There is a general list of abbreviations below, but if a pattern has any special abbreviations which apply only to that garment, then they are written at the beginning of that particular pattern.

Where a pattern has a chart or charts, there will be special instructions in the pattern to which it applies. There is also a general section on using the charts in this book, which is on page 61, and which it is important to read before beginning any charted knitting.

Abbreviations

K = Knit; P = Purl; st(s) = stitch(es); inc. = increase; dec. = decrease; beg. = beginning; cont. = continue; foll. = follow(ing); tbl. = through back of loop; sl. = slip; psso. = pass slip stitch over; yon. = yarn over needle; rem. = remaining; tog. = together; patt. = pattern; m1 = make 1 (i.e. lift the strand of yarn between the needles, place it on the left-hand needle and work into the back of it); rep. = repeat; alt. = alternate; rev.st.st = reverse stocking stitch.

1 Geometric Mohair

Picking up stitches

Most patterns at some stage or other require the knitter to pick
up stitches, usually round the neck opening to begin the
neck-band. Often knitters are very dissatisfied with the finish
they achieve when doing this, and it can spoil an otherwise
pleasing jumper.

There are various things which you can do to make this job
both easier and neater. Begin by looking at the way in which you
decrease to shape the neck edge. Sometimes a pattern will tell
you how. If it does not, it will probably simply say 'decrease at
the neck edge'. When decreasing, if you knit two stitches
together in the ordinary way, you will find that you have
achieved an almost invisible decrease at the right hand edge of
your work, but that there is an ugly visible crossed stitch at the
left-hand edge, which will show badly at one side of the
neckband when the garment is complete. To avoid this, when
decreasing at the left-hand edge of the work (looking at it with
the right side facing you), work the two stitches together at this
edge through the back of the loop, usually abbreviated tbl. That
is, place the point of the working needle through the back of both
stitches instead of, as normally, through the front. This crosses
the stitches the other way and makes the sides symmetrical and
the decreasing invisible.

Once you have your neat edges, what is the best way to pick
up the stitches from them? Most patterns give you an order for
picking up stitches, usually beginning with the back neck, and
also tell you to knit them at the same time. Instead, using a very
small needle size, which is much easier anyway, pick up the
stitches in the opposite direction without knitting them, and with
the wrong side facing. Then, using the correct needle size, with

the right side of the work facing and therefore working in the order stated in the pattern, knit the picked-up stitches from the very small needle. This gives you the opportunity to adjust the numbers, and to ensure that the stitches are evenly picked up.

If you find that your picking up produces a row of loose stitches that become holes, by knitting into the back of these you will twist the stitches and close the holes.

All of these remedies together should help to ensure that your picked-up edges do justice to the rest of your knitting.

Geometric Mohair

Materials

Spectrum Pirouette Mohair in:
Grey Dusk: 7(8,10) × 25g balls
Yellow Sunshine: 6(6,7) × 25g balls
Red Sunset: 6(6,7) × 25g balls
Sapphire Blue: 6(6,7) × 25g balls

1 pr. 5mm (No. 6) needles, 1 pr. 4mm (No. 8) needles.

Measurements

To fit:	Small	Medium	Large
Actual measurement:	35	42	49in
	89	107	124cm
Length (approx.):	23	23	23in
	58	58	58cm
Underarm length (approx.):	17½	17½	17½in
	44	44	44cm

Key to Chart

X = contrast
All other squares = background colour.

○ = bobble in CONTRAST.
To make bobble, work 3 times into marked st, turn and P3, turn and K3, turn and P3, turn and K3 tog.

– – – – – – – – = background colour divisions

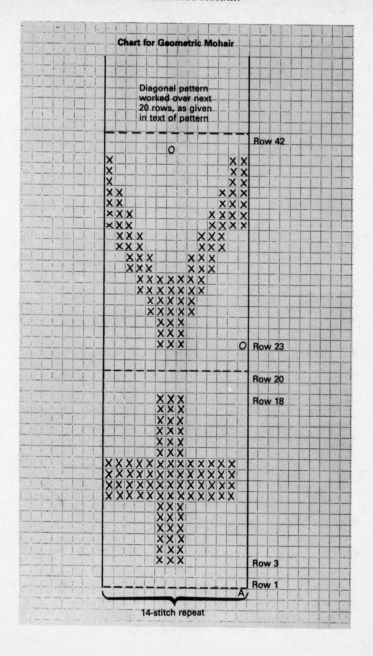

Chart for Geometric Mohair

Diagonal pattern
worked over next
20 rows, as given
in text of pattern

14-stitch repeat

7

Tension

16sts and 21 rows = 10cm (4in) on 5mm (No. 6) needles over
    st.st. and colour pattern.

Back

Using 4mm needles and grey, cast on 64(76,84)sts and work:
Row 1 – K1,(K2,P2) to last 3sts,K3.
Row 2 – K1,(P2,K2) to last 3sts,P2,K1
Rep. these 2 rows until rib measures 5cm ending with row 1.
Next (increasing) row – Keeping rib correct, *rib 9(8,5),m1*,
    rep. from * to * to last 1(4,9)st(s), rib to end. (71,85,99sts)
Change to 5mm needles and yellow, and using st.st. work rows 1
    and 2 of the chart.
Now work rows 3–18 of the chart, using grey as the contrast on a
    yellow background, working the 14st. rep. across the work
    until 1st. remains, work this st. as the st. marked A on the
    chart again, so making the work symmetrical.
Work rows 19 and 20 in plain yellow.
Work rows 21 and 22 in plain blue.
Work from the chart as before working rows 23–41 using yellow
    as a contrast on a blue background and working bobbles as
    marked in contrast, but omitting bobbles on the two
    extreme-edge sts.
Work row 42 in plain blue.
Work 2 rows of plain red.
Next row (Row 45 of the pattern) – *K3 red,K3 blue*, rep. from
    * to * to last 5(1,3)sts,K3(1,3) red,K2(0,0) blue.
Row 46 – P3(0,1) blue,P2(1,2) red *,P1 red,P3 blue,P2 red*,
    rep. from * to * to end.
Row 47 – *K1 red,K3 blue,K2 red*, rep from * to * to last
    5(1,3)sts,K1(1,1) red,K3(0,2) blue,K1(0,0) red.
Row 48 – P2(0,0) red, P3(1,3) blue, *P3 red,P3 blue,* rep. from
    * to * to end.
Cont. in this way, moving the 3st-wide diagonal bars 1st. over on
    every row until 16 rows of this diagonal stripe pattern have
    been worked.
Work 2 plain red rows so completing one 62-row repeat of the
    pattern.
Repeat the pattern rows again, but in the following colours:
Rows 1 to 20 – Grey background, red contrast.
Rows 21 to 42 – Yellow background, grey contrast.

Working in the same colour as on the previous row, work the
next row:
Cast off 24(30,36)sts,K until 24(30,36)sts rem., place the
23(25,27)sts just worked on to a holder, cast off to end.

Front

Work as given for back, working in the same pattern and colour
sequence, until front is 16 rows shorter than the back, so
ending with a P row. Cont. to keep colours and pattern
correct throughout remainder of work, shape neck:
Next row – Pattern 30(36,42), turn, P2 tog tbl, pattern to end.
** Dec. 1st. at neck edge only on next 2 rows, then on every alt.
row until 24(30,36)sts rem.
Work straight until front matches back to shoulder.
Cast off. **

Rejoin yarn to inside edge of rem. sts, pattern 11(13,15)sts and
place them on a holder, pattern to end.
Next row – Pattern to last 2,P2 tog.
Rep from ** to **.

Sleeves

With 4mm needles and using grey, cast on 36(36,40)sts and work
5cm in rib in the same way as given for the back, ending
with row 2, and inc. by 7(7,3)sts evenly across the last row.
(43,43,43sts)
Change to 5mm needles and st.st. and work in the same colour
and pattern sequence as given for the back and front, at the
same time, keeping patterns and colours correct throughout
all shaping, inc. 1st. at each end of the 5th and every foll.
5th(4th,3rd) row until there are 73(81,89)sts.
Work straight until 82 rows have been worked in all, (i.e. the 62
pattern rows once, then rows 1–20 once more).
Cast off loosely in the same colour as that of the previous row.

Neckband

Join left shoulder seam. With 4mm needles and using grey, and
with right side facing, pick up and K the 23(25,27)sts from
the back neck holder, 13(15,15)sts down the left neck slope,

the 11(13,15)sts from the front neck holder, and 13(15,15)sts
up the right neck slope. (60,68,72sts)

Starting with row 2, work 6 rows of rib in the same way as
before.

Cast off very loosely in rib.

To Make Up

Do not press or brush.

Join rem. seams matching pattern and ensuring that armholes are
23(25,28)cm deep after making up.

2 Shoulder Ridge Jumper

Making up

So many people have problems in sewing their jumpers together
after they are knitted. Some people hate doing it, and have
cupboards full of jumper pieces which they can't face
assembling. Others do make their garments up but are very
unhappy with the results. There are several things which you can
do to make this job easier, and much more satisfying.

Many modern yarns have 'Do not Press' written on the ball
band. So, please don't. It really does ruin them. Instead block
the pieces, that is pin them out to shape, on a padded surface
such as a special board or even the carpet, and then spray them
with water using a garden spray (clean, of course). When they
are completely dry they can be removed and are ready to sew
together.

Always pin knitted pieces ends together first, then middles
together, and then the middles of the spaces, and so on, so that
the stretchy knitting is evenly linked. Make sure that you have
matched any shapings, colours or patterns.

Ideally, if your knitted edges are neat enough, they should
be joined edge to edge with an invisible stitch like ladder stitch.
But, ordinarily, the best way of seaming knitting for practical
purposes is backstitch, which will stretch with the knitting. Only
oversew if the knitting is very thick, for example work done in
garter stitch.

Always use a blunt tapestry sewing needle with a big eye, as
this is much easier to thread, and does not split the yarn.

If you have been knitting with a very fluffy or textured yarn,
especially one that is a bouclé or a lumpy fashion yarn, you will
find it much easier to use a matching double knitting or even a
4-ply yarn to sew up with. If you have nothing that matches, buy

a skein of tapestry wool in the right colour and use that.

Practise your making-up skills on this simple black-and-white raglan sleeved jumper, which has ridged shoulders made by working a very easy stitch pattern.

Shoulder Ridge Jumper

Materials

Spectrum Niagara Double Knit in:
White: 5(6,6,7) × 100g balls
Black: 1(1,1,1) × 100g ball

1 pr. 4mm (No. 8) needles, 1 pr. 3¼mm (No. 10) needles.

Measurements

To fit:	34	36	38	40in
	86	91	97	102cm
Actual measurements:	38	40	42	44in
	97	102	107	112cm
Length:	24	25	25	25in
	61	63	63	63cm
Underarm length:	17½	18	18	18in
	44	46	46	46cm

Tension

22sts and 30 rows = 10cm (4in) on 4mm (No. 8) needles over
st.st.

Ridge Pattern

Row 1 – K. (Marking each end of this row.)
Row 2 – P.
Rows 3,5,7,9 and 11 – K.
Rows 4,6,8,10 and 12 – P.
Row 13 – K.
Row 14 – *with the point of the right-hand needle, pick up the
loop of the first st. of row 1 (the marked row). Place it on the
left-hand needle, and P tog this loop and the first st. of row
14*, rep. from * to * with every st., so purling tog the sts
from row 1 with those of row 14, until no sts. from row 1
rem. unworked, so completing the double row, and making
rows 1–14 into a ridge on the right side of the work.
Rows 15,17 and 19 – K.
Rows 16,18 and 20 – P.
Rows 1–20 are repeated throughout the ridge st. pattern.

13

Back

Using 3¼mm needles and white, cast on 99(105,111,115)sts and
  work:
Row 1 – K1,(K1,P1) to last 2sts,K2.
Row 2 – K1,(P1,K1) to end.
Rep. these 2 rows until rib measures 6cm ending with a row 2,
  and increasing by 6(6,4,6)sts evenly across the last row.
  (105,111,115,121sts)
Change to 4mm needles and st.st. starting with a K row, and
  work straight to a total measurement of 38(41,39,39)cm
  ending with a P row.

Shape armholes:
Cast off 4(5,6,7)sts at beg. of next 2 rows. (97,101,103,107sts)

Shape raglan:
Next row – K2 tog,K to last 2sts,K2 tog tbl.
Next row – P. **
Rep. these 2 rows until 31(33,33,35)sts rem. Leave these sts on a
  holder.

Front

Work as given for back as far as **.
Rep. the 2 raglan shaping rows until 47(49,49,51)sts rem.

Shape neck and raglan:
Next row – K2 tog,K12,K2 tog tbl, turn, leaving rem. sts on a
  holder, P2 tog tbl,P to end.
*** Cont. to dec. at raglan edge in the same way as before on
  every alt. row, at the same time, dec. 1st. at neck edge on
  next 2 rows, then on every alt. row 4 times. (2sts rem.)
Work 2 tog.
Fasten off. ***
Place centre 15(17,17,19)sts on a holder.
Rejoin yarn to inside edge of rem. 16sts and work next row:
K2 tog,K12,K2 tog tbl.
Next row – P to last 2sts,P2 tog.
Rep from *** to ***.

Sleeves

Using 3¼mm needles and white, cast on 45(47,49,51)sts and
  work 6cm in rib in the same way as given for the back,

ending with row 2.

Change to 4mm needles and st.st. starting with a K row, inc. 1st. at each end of the 3rd, then every foll. 4th row until there are 99(99,105,105)sts.

Work straight to a total measurement of 44(46,46,46)cm ending with a P row.

Shape armholes:

Cast off 4(5,6,7)sts at beg. of next 2 rows. (91,89,93,91sts)

Work ridge pattern and shape raglan top together:

Complete remainder of work in ridge pattern, working rows 1–14 in black, then rows 15–20 in white, then rows 1–20 in white.

Rep. these 40 rows throughout the remainder of the sleeve, so working alt. black and white ridges, at the same time, shape the raglan as follows, shaping in rows 15–20 of the pattern only, so that the shaping occurs only in the 'background' and the ridges are worked straight.

Dec. 1st. at each end of the next and every foll. alt. row of the 'background' in the same way as on the back and front until there are 57(49,53,45)sts.

Cont. to keep ridge pattern correct, dec. 1st. at each end of every row until 5sts rem.

Leave these sts on a holder.

Neckband

Do not press.

Seam left back, and left- and right-front raglan seams, matching shapings, stitching together the main 'background' only and not catching down the ends of the ridges, or seaming them in any way.

With 3¼mm needles and white, with right side facing, pick up and K the 31(33,33,35)sts from the back neck holder, working 2 tog in the middle, 5sts from the left sleeve head, 16sts down the left neck slope, the 15(17,17,19)sts from the front neck holder, 16sts up the right front slope, and the 5sts from the right sleeve head. (87,91,91,95sts)

Starting with row 2, work 8 rows of rib in the same way as before.

Cast off loosely in rib.

To Make Up

Join rem. seams (not seaming the ends of the ridges in any way).

15

3 Nostalgic Jumper

Adapting pattern size

So often knitters find just the pattern they want, but it is the wrong size, especially if it is one of the beautiful old patterns that are such a feature of this book.

The lovely 1940s pattern illustrated here, which I adapted as the Nostalgic jumper, was originally in only one size, and the following text was added to the pattern to cope with just this problem. The method of altering sizes described here is equally applicable to today's patterns.

How to alter standard sizes

1. Divide the extra amount needed for the bust measurement by two, adding half to the front and half to the back, calculating the number of stitches from the tension.
2. At the armhole shaping, add half of the additional stitches to each shoulder, leaving neck and armholes the same, and divide the additional stitches evenly along the casting off.
3. Usually with O.S. garments the front is required two or three inches longer than the back. Simplify this by turning after the welt is knitted to give extra fullness to the front.

It is unlikely that you will want to follow instruction number 3. It means adding extra rows centrally by turning before the end of the rows as one does when shaping a sock heel. This would give a very unfashionable 'pouter pigeon' shape which was right in (or rather out), at the time.

Instructions 1 and 2 are ideal though. In effect what you would do is to check how many stitches per cm you have in your tension, for example 20sts per 10cm = 2sts per cm.

If you would like to knit the garment one size bigger, you

Inset: the original pattern leaflet.

will want to add about 6cms, that is 12sts. If you are adding half to the back, and half to the front, that becomes 6sts each, which will be added as 3sts each side of each piece of work.

Keep the neck and armhole shapes the same, leaving your 3sts per side to carry on up to the shoulder, then cast them off evenly across each side. For example if your pattern requires that you cast off three lots of 7sts for your shoulder, then you will cast off three lots of 8sts.

The same principle will apply to any size alterations, and if you wish to make a pattern smaller, simply reverse the process.

The old pattern used here makes the garment shape in what is, to us, a very unconventional way. The back is much narrower than the front, and the neckband is added in two halves. But the resulting garment shape is beautifully tailored and very satisfying to knit. The original black is still just as fashionable as it ever was, as is the authentic Forties shape.

Nostalgic Jumper

Materials

Spectrum Vermont Perle/4 ply in:
Black: 3(3) × 100g balls

1 pr. 3¼mm (No. 10) needles, 1 pr. 3mm (No. 11) and 1 pr. 2¾mm (No. 12) needles.

Measurements

To fit:	32–34	36–38in
	81–86	91–97cm

Actual measurement: Because this jumper has a narrow back and gathered front, the actual measurement is not an accurate guide to its fit, but the sizes fit up to 34in and up to 38in with a fitting waist and comfortable ease.

Length:	19½	19½in
	50	50cm
Underarm seam:	3½	3½in
	9	9cm

Tension

28sts and 36 rows = 10cm (4in) on 3¼mm (No. 10) needles over st.st.

Back

Using 3¼mm needles, cast on 100(116)sts.
Change to 2¾mm needles and work 13cm in K1,P1 rib.
Change to 3mm needles and work 6cm in K1,P1 rib.*
Change to 3¼mm needles and cont. in st.st. until work measures 33cm.

Shape armholes:
K2 tog at beg. of the next 10(12) rows. (90,104sts) Cont. without shaping until work measures 50cm ending with K row.

Shape neck and shoulders:
Next row – P30(36) turn, cast off 5(6), knit back.
Cont. on these 25(30)sts, cast off 5(6)sts at beg. of each row until all sts are cast off.
Slip centre 30(32)sts on to a holder.
Rejoin yarn to inside edge of rem. sts, cast off 5(6), P to end.
Rep. from ** to ** but leave final st. on the needle, do not fasten off.
With right side of work facing, remaining on larger needles, pick up and K15(17) further sts down the right back neck slope, K the 30(32)sts from the holder and 16(18)sts up the left back neck slope. 62(68sts)
*** Work 4 rows of K1,P1 rib.
Cont. in rib, change to 3mm needles and rib 6 further rows, change to 2¾mm needles and rib 10 further rows. (20 rib rows in total)
Cast off in rib. ***

Sleeves

Same for both sizes.
Using 3mm needles, cast on 80sts and work 20 rows in K1,P1 rib.

Commence gathered section:

First row – (K1,inc.in this st.)24 times, (K1,P1)16 times, (inc.in the next st.)24 times. (128sts)

2nd row – P48,(K1,P1)16 times,P48.

3rd row – K48,inc.in the next 2sts,(K1,P1)14 times, inc. in the next 2sts,K48.

4th row – P52,(K1,P1)14 times,P52.

5th row – K52,inc.in the next 2sts,(K1,P1)12 times, inc. in the next 2sts,K52.

6th row – P56,(K1,P1)12 times,P56.

7th row – K56,inc.in the next 2sts,(K1,P1)10 times, inc. in the next 2sts,K56.

8th row – P60,(K1,P1)10 times,P60.

9th row – K60,inc.in the next 2sts,(K1,P1)8 times, inc. in the next 2sts,K60.

10th row – P64,(K1,P1)8 times,P64.

11th row – K64,inc.in the next 2sts,(K1,P1)6 times, inc. in the next 2sts,K64.

12th row – P68,(K1,P1)6 times,P68.

13th row – K68,inc.in the next 2sts,(K1,P1)4 times, inc. in the next 2sts,K68.

14th row – P72,(K1,P1)4 times,P72.

15th row – K72,inc.in the next 2sts,(K1,P1)twice, inc. in the next 2sts,K72.

16th row – P76,K1,P1,K1,P77. (156sts)

Shape head of sleeve:

Change to 3¼mm needles, and cont. in st.st., K2 tog at both ends of every row until work measures 24cm, then cast off.

Front

Work exactly as given for back as far as *.

Commence gathered section.

First row – K10(18), then rep. first row of gathered section in sleeve, K10(18). (148,164sts)

2nd row – P10(18), then rep. 2nd row of gathered section in sleeve, P10(18).

Cont. thus as gathered section of sleeves, with 10(18)sts in st.st. at each end for 14 more rows. (176,192sts)

Change to 3¼mm needles and cont. in st.st. until work measures 33cm.

Shape armholes:

K2 tog at each end of next 10(11) rows. (156,170sts)

Cont. without shaping until work measures 43cm ending with a
    K row.

Shape neck:

Next row – P57(63),P3 tog, turn, P3 tog, knit back.

Cont. on these 56(62)sts, working P3 tog at neck edge on each
    row until 18(24)sts rem., then cast off.

Slip centre 36(38)sts on to a holder, rejoin yarn to inside edge of
    rem. sts, P3 tog,P57(63).

Cont. on these 58(64)sts, working P3 tog at neck edge of every
    row until 18(24)sts rem., then cast off.

With right side of work facing, remaining on larger needles, pick
    up and K30(30)sts down left neck slope, K2 tog across
    36(38)sts on the holder, and pick up and K30(31)sts up right
    neck slope. (78,80sts)

Work as given for back from *** to ***.

To Make Up

Do not press.

Join shoulder and neckband seams, draw up sleevehead to fit
    armhole and seam into position, with most of the fullness
    around the shoulder seam.

Join side and sleeve seams matching shaping and rib.

N.B. The front of the jumper is shorter than the back, to give the
    neckband its distinctive shape.

4 Stitch Sampler Jumper

Welts and ribs

A common problem with knitted garments is dissatisfaction with the welts and ribs. Some people find that their jumpers have very loose sloppy welts which look untidy, others have ribs which cut off their circulation, especially around necklines. Both these problems have a solution.

One of the more simple ways of tightening up ribs is to work them on needles three sizes smaller than the main needles, rather than the usual two. Knit two, purl two rib, or even knit three, purl three, also draws the bottom of the garment in more than the usual knit one, purl one.

If neither of these solutions is sufficient, then experiment with knitting in elastic. This is very fine, almost invisible elastic which can be bought from wool shops, and which is worked together with the yarn into the ribs. Be careful to use it unstretched. It needs simply to lie alongside the yarn as you work, otherwise it will either tighten the rib too drastically, or loop untidily on the surface.

If you find that your ribs are too tight, then this is probably caused by the casting off, rather than the actual ribbed knitting. To correct this simply cast off on a much larger needle, or, for neckbands, don't cast off at all. Instead, work twice as much rib as you need, perhaps with a wrong side knit row in the middle as a fold line. Turn the neckband on to the wrong side and then, being very careful to catch every stitch, loosely and evenly sew the stitches down to the beginning of the neckband with a very stretchy embroidery stitch like herringbone. This is especially helpful for jumpers for small children, who have proportionately larger heads, but who need snug fitting necklines.

Children's garments are also more prone to wear, and need

to grow with their owners. To help with these problems, knit the welt rib in the usual way and then cast it off loosely. Turn it upside down and pick up the cast-ON edge, working the garment from now on, from this edge, in the usual way. This means that as the child grows, or wears out welts, especially cuffs, they are very much easier to replace, extend, or repair. A new welt will even look good added in this way in a contrast yarn, which is useful if you have none of the original colour left over.

The stitch sampler jumper here has ribs both at the top and the welt, and was knitted in a pale and pretty lilac.

> Each evening my wife Betty sits
> In front of the telly and knits.
> If the viewing's compulsive
> The garment's repulsive.
> If the programmes are dull, then it fits.
>
> CONTRIBUTED BY MR RUSSELL

Stitch Sampler Jumper

Materials

Spectrum Detroit Double Knit in:
Lilac Bluebird 5 × 100g balls

1 pr. 4mm (No. 8) needles, 1 pr. 3¼mm (No. 10) needles.

Measurements

One size only, fits up to: 40in (102cm)

Actual measurement: 44in (112cm)

Length (approx.): 25in (63cm)

Sleeve underarm: 17½in (44cm)

Tension

22sts and 30 rows = 10cm (4in) on 4mm (No. 8) needles over st.st.

Back and Front (both alike)
Using 3¼mm needles, cast on 109sts and work:
Row 1 – K1,(K1,P1) to last 2sts,K2.
Row 2 – K1,(P1,K1) to end.
Rep. these 2 rows until rib measures 6cm ending with row 1.
Next row – Cont. to keep rib correct, inc:
Rib 11,*m1,rib 7*, rep. from * to * to last 7, rib to end. (122sts)
Change to 4mm needles and commence pattern:
Row 1 – P2,K28,P2,(K4,P4)3 times,K4,P2,(K1,P1)14 times,P2,K28,P2.
Row 2 – K2,P28,K2,(P1,K1)14 times,K2,P3,(K4,P4)3 times,K3,P28,K2.
Row 3 – P2,K28,P4,(K4,P4)3 times,K2,P2,(K1,P1)14 times,P2,K28,P2.
Row 4 – K2,P28,K2,(P1,K1)14 times,K2,P1,(K4,P4)3 times,K5,P28,K2.
Row 5 – P2,K28,P6,(K4,P4)3 times,P2,(K1,P1)14 times,P32.
Row 6 – K32,(P1,K1)14 times,K5,(P4,K4)3 times,P1,K2,P28,K2.
Row 7 – P2,K28,P2,K2,(P4,K4)3 times,P4,(K1,P1)14 times,P32.
Row 8 – K32,(P1,K1)14 times,K3,(P4,K4)3 times,P3,K2,P28,K2.
Rows 9 to 16 – Rep. rows 1 to 8.
Rows 17 to 20 – Rep. rows 1 to 4.
Row 21 – P17,(K4,P4)3 times,K4,P2,K28,P2,(K1,P1)14 times,P17.
Row 22 – K17,(K1,P1)14 times,K2,P28,K3,(P4,K4)3 times,P3,K17.
Row 23 – P17,K2,(P4,K4)3 times,P4,K28,P2,K28,P17.
Row 24 – K80,(P4,K4)3 times,P1,K17.
Row 25 – P21,(K4,P4)3 times,P2,(yon,K2 tog)14 times,P2,(K1,P1) 14 times,P17.
Row 26 – K17,(K1,P1)14 times,K32,P1,(K4,P4)3 times,K20.
Row 27 – P19,(K4,P4)3 times,K2,P2,K28,P2,K28,P17.
Row 28 – K47,P28,K2,P3,(K4,P4)3 times,K18.
Rows 29 to 36 – Rep. rows 21 to 28.

Rows 37 to 40 – Rep. rows 21–24.

Row 41 – P2,K28,P2,(K1,P1)14 times,P2,K4,(P4,K4)3 times,P2,K28,P2.

Row 42 – K2,P28,K2,P3,(K4,P4)3 times,K3,(P1,K1)14 times,K2,P28,K2.

Row 43 – P2,K28,P2,(K1,P1)14 times,P4,(K4,P4)3 times,K2,P2, K28,P2.

Row 44 – K2,P28,K2,P1,(K4,P4)3 times,K5,(P1,K1)14 times,K2,P28,K2.

Row 45 – P32,(K1,P1)14 times,P6,(K4,P4)3 times,P2,K28,P2.

Row 46 – K2,P28,K5,(P4,K4)3 times,P1,K2,(P1,K1)14 times,K32.

Row 47 – P32,(K1,P1)14 times,P2,K2,(P4,K4)3 times,P4,K28,P2.

Row 48 – K2,P28,K3,(P4,K4)3 times,P3,K2,(P1,K1)14 times,K32.

Rows 49 to 56 – Rep. rows 41 to 48.

Rows 57 to 60 – Rep. rows 41 to 44.

Row 61 – K15,P2,(K1,P1)14 times,P32,K4,(P4,K4)3 times,P2,K15.

Row 62 – P15,K3,(P4,K4)3 times,P3,K32,(K1,P1)14 times,K2,P15.

Row 63 – K15,P2,K28,P32,K2,(P4,K4)3 times,P4,K15.

Row 64 – K20,(P4,K4)3 times,P1,K77.

Row 65 – K1,(yon,K2 tog)7 times,P2,(K1,P1)14 times,P36, (K4,P4)3 times, P2,K1,(yon,K2 tog)7 times.

Row 66 – K17,P1,(K4,P4)3 times,K35,(K1,P1)14 times,K17.

Row 67 – K15,P2,K28,P34,(K4,P4)3 times,K2,P2,K15.

Row 68 – P15,K2,P3,(K4,P4)3 times,K63,P15.

Rows 69 to 76 – Rep. rows 61 to 68.

Rows 77 to 80 – Rep. rows 61 to 64.

Rep. rows 1 to 80 once more. (160 pattern rows worked in all.)

Remaining on larger needles, inc. 1st. at beg. of first row (123sts), and starting with row 1, work 6cm in rib in the same way as given for the welt.

Cast off.

Sleeves

With 3¼mm needles, cast on 49sts and work 6cm in rib in the

same way as given for the back and front welts ending with
row 2, and inc. by 6sts evenly across this last row. (55sts)
Change to 4mm needles and st.st. starting with a K row, and inc.
1st. at each end of the 3rd and every foll. 4th row until there
are 111sts.
Work straight to a total length of 44cm.
Cast off.

To Make Up

Do not press.
Join shoulder seams leaving a 23cm-wide central neck opening.
Join rem. seams, matching pattern and ensuring that the
armholes are 25cm deep after making up.

An early knitted bear.

5 Jumper with Fair Isle V Neck

Fair Isle knitting

The traditional Fair Isle knitting patterns always use only two colours on any one row, and only have two, three, or at the most four stitches of any one colour together. If you look at such patterns you will see that larger runs of stitches are broken by a spot of the contrast colour. This is because, although they were decorative patterns, they also had to be knitted quickly out of sheer economic necessity, by folk who were on survival piece-work rates.

This means that in Fair Isle knitting you are actually meant to strand the yarn which is not in use across the back of the contrast stitches. This is unlike picture knitting, where several colours are used on one row, and often in quite large blocks, without any stranding across the back.

When working in Fair Isle take care not to pull the contrast yarn strands tight across the back, as this looks lumpy and spoils the stretchiness of the knitting. Almost everyone, however, pulls Fair Isle knitting in a little, so it is a good idea to work a tension square in your pattern, and to choose a needle size for it which will achieve the same tension as the plain-coloured stocking stitch. You can then use this probably larger needle for the Fair Isle rows only, and so keep the shape and fabric of your knitting consistent.

This jumper, like the last, has a nostalgic feeling, although it is a modern design. The yarn is a luxury alpaca, which feels lovely. The Fair Isle is worked in the very deep V as one would the colours of a cricket sweater, and the correct tension will make it fit just as it should.

Jumper with Fair Isle V Neck

Materials

Spectrum Atlanta Alpaca Double Knit in:
Main Colour 'MC' Natural: 10(11,12,12) × 50g balls
Contrast 'A' Mid Grey, Contrast 'B' Mid Brown and Contrast 'C'
White: 1 ball of each for all sizes.

1 pr. 4mm (No.8) needles, 1 pr. 3¼ mm (No.10) needles.
Additional needle sizes may be required – see Tension.

Measurements

To fit:	34	36	38	40in
	86	91	97	102cm
Actual measurement:	38	40	42	44in
	97	102	107	112cm
Length (approx):	25	26	26	26in
	63	66	66	66cm
Underarm length:	17½	18	18	18½in
	44	46	46	47cm

Tension

22sts and 30 rows = 10cm (4in) on 4mm (No. 8) needles over
st.st. N.B. Ensure that stitch tension over Fair Isle pattern is
the same as standard tension, working Fair Isle rows on
larger needles if necessary.

Front

Using 3¼mm needles and MC, cast on 99(105,111,115)sts and
work in rib:
Row 1 – K2,(P1,K1) to last st.,K1.
Row 2 – K1,(P1,K1) to end.
Rep. these 2 rows until rib measures 10cm ending with row 2,
and inc. by 6(6,4,6)sts evenly across the last row.
(105,111,115,121sts).
Change to 4mm needles and st.st. starting with a K row.★★
Work straight to a total length of 23(25,25,25)cm ending with a P
row.

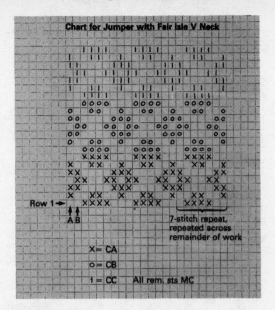

Divide for V neck:

Next row – K50(53,55,58)sts,K2 tog tbl., turn, leaving rem.sts on a holder, P to end.

Next row – K.

Next row – P2 tog tbl., P to end.

Next row – K.

Next row – P.

Next row – K to last 2sts,K2 tog tbl.

Next row – P.

***Rep. these 6 rows until 2(5,7,10)sts rem, at the same time, when front measures a total length of 41(42,42,41)cm, to shape armholes, cast off 12sts at armhole edge.

When shaping is complete, cast off.***

Return to sts on holder, rejoining yarn to inside edge, and place the first (centre) st. on to a pin, K2 tog,K to end.

Next row – P.

Next row – K.

Next row – P to last 2sts,P2 tog.

Next row – K.

Next row – P.

Next row – K2 tog,k to end.

Work as given for other side from *** to ***.

31

Front V

With 4mm needles and using MC, pick up and K, with right side
    facing, 92sts down the left neck slope, the 1st. from the
    safety pin, and 92sts up the right neck slope. (185sts)
Change to needles chosen for Fair Isle if necessary.
Next row – In P, work row 1 of the chart, reading from left to
    right, starting at A, then working from the chart to 2sts
    before the marked st. on pin, P2 tog in MC (these will both
    be MC sts), P the st. from the pin in MC, P2 tog tbl. in MC
    (these 2 sts are the A and B sts), then work from the chart to
    the end.
Next row – Keeping row 2 of chart correct by referring to the
    row before, K2 tog, pattern to 2sts before st. on the pin, K2
    tog tbl, in MC,K1 in MC,K2 tog in MC, pattern to last 2sts,
    K2 tog tbl.
Next row – Keeping row 3 of chart correct, pattern to 2sts before
    marked st.,P2 tog in MC, P1 in MC,P2 tog tbl. in MC,
    pattern to end.
Rep. these 2 rows of decreasing throughout the remainder of the
    chart, so working 21 pattern rows in all, and ending with a P
    row.
Change to needles chosen for normal st.st. if necessary, K1 row,
    then P1 row in MC only, dec. on these rows also as before.
    (117sts)
Leave sts on a spare needle or holders.

Back

Work as for front as far as **.
Work straight until back matches front to armhole ending with a
    P row.

Shape armholes:
Cast off 12sts at beg. of next 2 rows. (81,87,91,97sts)
Work straight until back matches front to shoulder, ending with
    a P row.
Next row – Cast off 24(27,29,32)sts, K until 24(27,29,32)sts
    rem., place the 33sts just worked on to a holder, cast off to
    end.

A typical and beautiful 1940s knitting pattern.

Sleeves

With 3¼mm needles and MC, cast on 45(49,49,53)sts and work
8cm in rib in the same way as given for the back, ending
with row 1, and inc. by 5(1,1,4)sts evenly over the last row.
(50,50,50,57sts).

Change to needles chosen for Fair Isle and st.st. starting with a P
row, and work this row as row 1 of the chart, reading from
left to right and starting at A. Cont. to work in Fair Isle
until chart is completed, then change to 4mm needles and
plain MC. AT THE SAME TIME, working all shaping into
the pattern, inc. 1st. at each end of the 3rd, then every foll.
3rd row until there are 100(106,106,111)sts.

Work straight to a total measurement of 44(46,46,47)cm, mark
each end of last row.

Work 16 further rows straight, cast off loosely.

Neck Rib

Retaining the front V on the needles or holders, join the left
    shoulder seam.
With 3¼mm needles and MC, with right side facing, work the
    sts from the back neck holder:
K1,(K1,P1) to end of back neck holder, then work (K1,P1)
    down the sts of the left slope to 2sts before the centre front
    st.,K2 tog tbl.,K1,K2 tog,(P1,K1) to last 2sts up the right
    slope,K2 tog. (147sts)
Next row – Rib to 2sts before the centre front st.,P2 tog,P1,P2
    tog tbl, rib to end.
Next row – Rib to 2sts before the centre front st.,K2 tog
    tbl.,K1,K2 tog, rib to end.
Rep. these 2 rows twice more. (7 rib rows in total)
Cast off in rib, dec. in the same way as before on this row also.

To Make Up

Press according to ball band instructions.
Join rem. seams, joining sleeve seam as far as marker, then insert
    remainder of sleeve edge into corners of armhole shaping.

6 Summer Cotton Top

Knitting with cotton

Cotton knitting has become increasingly popular lately, and has
certainly come a long way since we all used to knit cotton
dishcloths in school. There are several things which you can do
to help you get a really good finish on cotton garments.

To begin with, be really sure that your tension is correct.
More than any other yarns, cottons will fall out of shape –
especially when you wash them – if the knitting is sloppy.

Talking of washing, cotton is heavy, especially when wet, so
do dry jumpers flat if you can.

If you really like a tight rib, try using knitting in elastic with
the yarn as you work, or use a size smaller needle than you
would normally consider. Do be careful with this particular
pattern though, as it is already close fitting around the waist, and
you may prefer not to gather it in any further.

This delightful summer top was designed by Nadia Jones,
and was one of the runners up in the ORACLE Knitting Design
competition. She chose orange as her main colour, with a bright
yellow contrast – perfect to go with that tan on the beach.

Summer Cotton Top

Materials

Spectrum Cool Cotton Hi-Lights in:
Orange: 4(5,6) × 50g balls
Yellow: 1(2,2) × 50g balls

1pr. 4mm (No. 8) needles, 1 pr. 3¾mm (No. 9) and 1 pr.
3¼mm (No. 10) needles

Measurements

To fit:	32–34	36–38	40–42in
	81–86	91–97	102–107cm
Actual measurement:	38	42	46in
	97	107	117cm
Length:	21	21	21in
	53	53	53cm

Tension

22sts and 30 rows = 10cm (4in) on 4mm (No.8) needles over
st.st.

Back and Front (both alike)

Using 3¼mm needles and orange, cast on 89(99,111)sts and
work:
Row 1 – K1,(K1,P1) to last 2sts,K2.
Row 2 – K1,(P1,K1) to end.
Rep. these 2 rows three more times. (8 rib rows in all)
Next row – Cont. to keep rib correct, rib 38(43,49)sts in orange,
rib 13sts in yellow, rib rem. 38(43,49)sts in orange.
Cont. to keep rib correct and colours as set on the previous row,
rib 13 further rows.
Next row – Cont. to keep rib correct, rib 31(36,42) in orange, rib
27 in yellow, rib rem. 31(36,42)sts in orange.
Cont. to keep rib correct and colours as set on the previous row,
rib 27 further rows, so ending with a rib row 2.
Change to 4mm needles and st.st. and work the foll. row:
Keeping colours as set on the previous row, K7(4,2),
m1,K3(4,5), rep. from * to * 8 times,K27, **K3(4,5),
m1**, rep. from ** to ** 8 times,K rem. 7(4,2)sts.
(105,115,127sts)
Cont. in st.st. and with colours as set on the previous row, work
7 further rows.
Next row – K31(36,42)sts in orange,K43sts in yellow,K
rem.31(36,42)sts in orange.
Keeping colours as set on the previous row, work 33 further
rows.

Summer Cotton Top,
original design by Nadia Jones.

Shape underarms:

In orange, cast on 12sts at beg. of the next row, work these 12,
   and the next 23(28,34)sts in orange, (35,40,46 orange sts in
   all) K59 in yellow, K rem. 23(28,34)sts in orange.

In orange, cast on 12sts at beg. of next row, then P these sts in
   orange and work across row in P in colours as set.
   (129,139,151sts)

Keeping colours as set on the previous row, work 32 further
   rows.

Next row – K27(32,38)sts in orange,K75sts in yellow, K
   rem.27(32)38)sts in orange.

Keeping colours as set on the previous row, work 13 further rows.

Shape neck:

Cont. to keep colours as set throughout remainder of work, work
   next row: K81(86,92)sts, place the last 33sts worked on to a
   holder, K rem.48(53,59)sts ***Working on the set of sts for
   one side of the garment only, work a further 17 rows.

Cast off in correct colours.***

Rejoin yarn to inside edge of rem. sts. Rep. from *** to ***.

Neckband (same for all sizes)

Join one shoulder seam matching colours. This then becomes the
   left shoulder seam.

Using 3¼mm needles and yellow, with right side facing, pick up
   and K, beg. at the right side of the back neck, 14sts down
   the right back neck side, marking the last of these sts, the
   33sts from the back neck holder, 14sts up the left back neck
   side marking the first of these sts, 13sts down the left front
   neck side, marking the last of these sts, the 33sts from the
   front neck holder, and 14sts up the right front neck side,
   marking the first of these sts. (121sts)

Next row – *K1, (P1,K1) to 2sts before the next marked st.,P2
   tog,P1,P2 tog*, rep. from * to * 3 times more,K1,(P1,K1)
   to end.

Next row – K1, *(K1,P1) to 2sts before the next marked st.,K2
   tog, K1,K2 tog, P1*, rep. from * to * 3 times more,(K1,P1)
   to last 2sts,K2.

Rep. these 2 rows once more. (4 rib rows in all)

Cast off in rib.

Armbands

Join rem. shoulder seam and neckband seam matching colours.
Armbands are both alike:
Using needles one size smaller than those chosen for main
tension, ie 3¾mm, with right side facing, and using orange,
pick up and K, evenly, 49sts across one half of the sleeve
edge and 50sts across the other half. (99sts) Starting with
row 2 of rib as given for the back, work 5 rows of rib. Cast
off in rib.

To Make Up

Do not press.
Join rem. seams matching shaping.

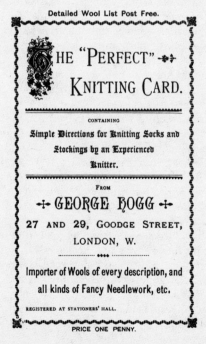

The front of the oldest pattern sent to ORACLE, *a Victorian
Knitting Card.*

7 Shawl Collared Mohair

Knitting and caring for mohair

Mohair is spun from the long silky coat of the Angora goat, and has become increasingly popular and fashionable. It can be very expensive, and so you will want to knit it with care, and also to look after your precious jumper well when it is finished.

Firstly, and especially if you are a less experienced knitter, do not choose a very difficult jumper pattern to knit in mohair to start with. This is partly because it is more difficult to see what you are doing because of the fluffiness of the yarn, but also because mohair is notoriously difficult to unpick, so that if you do make any mistakes you will find it hard to rectify them. If you have to unravel any mohair knitting do it slowly and as gently as you can, as drastic treatment will encourage moulting.

Secondly, try not to squash your knitting as you store it, whether finished or unfinished, as the beauty of mohair is its long downy texture.

When the garment is complete you can, if you wish, brush it. This was always done traditionally with a teazle, and they are still available, but more usually your wool shop will supply you with a specially made mohair brush. Brush firmly, but carefully, and you will find that you will have a very furry fabric. If you are unsure whether or not you will like the effect, try brushing your tension square first as an experiment.

Always wash mohair jumpers by hand, and in a special wash liquid which is designed for the purpose. Never use soap, and always wash in cool water, as both heat and soap cause felting. Rinse thoroughly but gently, and squeeze dry. A gentle spin dry will be successful, but never tumble dry as this is too drastic. Shake gently to raise the pile and dry flat. When dry, the mohair can again be gently brushed.

This spectacular shawl collared mohair jumper is in a gorgeous rich red, and was a runner up in the ORACLE Knitting Design competition. It was designed by Janet Knight, and is particularly simple to knit.

Shawl Collared Mohair,
original design by Janet Knight.

Shawl Collared Mohair

Materials

Spectrum Pirouette Mohair in:
Red Sunset: 19(21,23) × 25g balls

1 pr. 5mm (No. 6) needles, 1 pr. 4mm (No. 8) needles.
3 long circular needles, sizes 4mm, 4½mm and 5mm.

Measurements

To fit:	34–36	38– 40	42– 44in
	86–91	97–102	107–112cm
Actual measurement:	42	46	50in
	107	117	127cm
Length:	24	24	24in
	61	61	61cm
Underarm length:	17	17	17in
	43	43	43cm

Tension

16sts and 21 rows = 10cm (4in) on 5mm (No. 6) needles over
st.st.

Back

With 4mm needles cast on 72(80,88)sts and work:
Row 1 – K1,(K2,P2) to last 3sts,K3.
Row 2 – K1,(P2,K2) to last 3sts,P2,K1.
Rep. these 2 rows until rib measures 8cm ending with row 1.
Work the next, inc. row:
Keeping rib correct throughout, rib 3(4,2), *m1,rib 6(6,7)*, rep.
    from * to * to last 3(4,2)sts, smallest size only m1, all sizes,
    rib to end. (84,92,100sts)**
Change to 5mm needles and st.st. starting with a K row, and
    work straight to a total length of 58(58,58)cm ending with a
    P row.

Shape back neck:
Next row – K33 (37,41),K2 tog tbl., turn, P2 tog tbl.,P to end.

***Dec 1st. at neck edge only on next 4 rows.
Cast off rem. 29(33,37)sts.***
Place centre 14sts on a holder for back neck.
Rejoin yarn to inside edge of rem.sts,K2 tog,K to end.
Next row – P to last 2,P2 tog.
Rep from *** to ***.

Front

Work as given for back as far as **.

Divide for front opening:
Change to 5mm needles.
K 29(33,37)sts and place them on a holder, cast off 26sts, K rem.
    29(33,37).
Work straight in st.st. on these sts only until front matches back
    to shoulder, ending with a P row.
Cast off.
Rejoin yarn to rem. sts and work in st.st. to match first side, then
    cast off.

Sleeves (Both alike. The same for all sizes.)

Using 4mm needles, cast on 36sts and work 8cm in rib in the
    same way as given for the back, ending with row 1.
Next row – Keeping rib correct, rib 4,*m1, rib 3*, rep. from * to
    * to last 2sts, rib 2. (46sts)
Change to 5mm needles and st.st. and inc. 1st. at each end of the
    3rd, and every foll. 4th row until there are 68sts, then on
    every alt. row until there are 96sts.
Work 1 row.
Cast off loosely.

Neckband Rib

Join both shoulder seams. Using a 4mm, long circular needle,
    pick up and K, with right side facing, 84sts evenly up the
    complete right front edge, from immediately above the rib to
    the top, 9sts down the right back neck slope, the 14sts from
    the back neck holder, 9sts up the left back neck slope, and
    84sts evenly down the complete left front edge from the top
    to immediately above the rib. (200sts)

43

Starting with row 2, work in rib in the same way as given for the
back until this rib measures 5cm.
Change to a 4½mm circular needle and work a further 5cm in
rib.
Change to a 5mm circular needle and cont. in rib until rib
measures 19cm in all.
Cast off very loosely in rib.

To Make Up

Do not press.
Join rem. seams ensuring that armholes are 30cm deep after
making up. Catch down the two edges of the neck rib
evenly, right over left to the top of the gap at the front welt.

> There was a young lady from Lundy
> Who never would knit on a Sunday.
> In patterns unique
> She would knit all the week,
> But the Sabbath was Marathon Run Day.
>
> CONTRIBUTED BY D. V. S.

8 Lace Cardigan

Holes: lace knitting and buttonholes

Knitting lace is much easier than it looks, and the patterns,
although they seem long and detailed, are usually based simply
on a number of stitches worked in a repeating pattern. If you
have never knitted lace before, follow the instructions carefully
and begin slowly. You will soon speed up as you begin to learn
the pattern, and to follow the way in which it grows.

One of the commonest difficulties which knitters have with
lace patterns is that of shaping the work. Patterns often say,
'keeping lace pattern correct, shape:' and, especially if you are a
beginner, this is rather a daunting prospect.

To make it much easier, look carefully at your knitting and
the pattern and see how many stitches there are in each repeat.
Then, at each edge of the work, mark in some way the stitches
which make the outside repeat. For example, if you have a
sixteen-stitch repeat, place some kind of marker between the
sixteenth and seventeenth stitches in from each edge. You can
use odd scraps of contrast yarn, safety pins, paper clips or even
special coloured split rings which you can buy for the purpose.

Once your outer repeat is marked it is much easier to find
your way among the decreasings, so that if you have cast off three
stitches, you can see that you have thirteen stitches of your repeat
left, and can find where the patterns begin and end without
having to struggle with the whole row.

Buttonholes are usually made by casting off a number of
stitches on one row, and then replacing them with cast on
stitches on a subsequent row. To make a really neat buttonhole,
cast on one less stitch than you need on the second row, and
then, on the third row, pick up the loop which the casting on has
made at the beginning of the buttonhole, place it on the left-hand

needle and work into the back of it. This restores the correct number of stitches. It also closes the loop, which would otherwise remain to get in the way when the buttonhole is in use. The effect is much neater too.

This cardigan is knitted in a pretty peach pink, and has a large and attractive lace pattern, which makes an interesting reverse pattern with the spaces of plain knitting in between the lace.

Lace Cardigan

Materials

Spectrum Niagara Double Knit in:
Apricot: 5(6,6,7) × 100g balls.
7 Buttons

1 pr. 4mm (No. 8) needles and 1 pr. 3¼mm (No. 10) needles.

Measurements

To fit:	28–32	34–38	40–44	46–50in
	71–81	86–97	102–112	117–127cm
Actual measurement:	35	41	46	52in
	89	104	117	132cm
Length (approx):	23	24	24	25in
	58	61	61	63cm
Underarm length (approx):	17	17½	17½	18in
	43	44	44	46cm

Tension

22sts and 30 rows = 10cm(4in) on 4mm (No. 8) needles over st.st.

Special Abbreviations

yo 2 = yarn over needle twice; dec. L = sl 2sts separately K-wise to right-hand needle, put the tip of the left-hand needle through both loops of these sts from back to front and K together in this position.

Lace Pattern:

First row – (wrong side facing) K.

2nd and 3rd rows – K.

4th row – *K8,yo 2,K8*, rep. from * to * to end of row.

5th row – *P8,(K1,P1,K1,P1,K1) into loop made by yo 2, thus
  making 5sts, P8*, rep. from * to * to end of row.

6th row – *dec. L,K17,K2 tog*, rep. from * to * to end of row.

7th row – P.

8th row – *dec. L,K5,(yon,K1) 5 times,yon,K5,K2 tog*, rep.
  from * to * to end of row.

9th row – *P6,K11,P6*, rep. from * to * to end of row.

10th row – *dec. L.,K19,K2 tog*, rep. from * to * to end of row.

11th row – *P5,K11,P5*, rep. from * to * to end of row.

12th row – *dec, L,K2,(dec.L,yon) 3 times, K1,(yon,K2 tog) 3
  times,K2,K2 tog*, rep. from * to * to end of row.

13th row – *P4,K11,P4*, rep. from * to * to end of row.

14th row – *dec. L,K15,K2 tog*, rep. from * to * to end of row.

15th row – *P3,K11,P3*, rep. from * to * to end of row.

16th row – *(dec.L) twice,(yon,dec.L) twice,yon,K1,(yon,K2
  tog) 3 times,K2*, rep. from * to * to end of row.

Back

With 3¼mm needles, cast on 89(105,121,137)sts and work:

Row 1 – K1,(K1,P1) to last 2sts,K2.

Row 2 – K1,(P1,K1) to end.

Rep. these two rows until rib measures 5cm ending with row 1,
  and inc. by 7sts evenly across this last row.
  (96,112,128,144sts)

Change to 4mm needles and to lace pattern and work straight in
  pattern to a length of approx. 58(61,61,63)cm ending after a
  complete pattern rep., ie with 16th row of the pattern.

Next row – Cast off 32(32,48,48)sts, K until 32(32,48,48)sts
  remain, place the 32(48,32,48)sts just worked on to a holder,
  cast off to end.

Left Front

With 3¼mm needles, cast on 51(55,67,71)sts and work 5cm in
  rib in the same way as given for the back, inc. by 4sts evenly
  across the last row, a row 1. (55,59,71,75sts)

Next row – still using smaller needles, rib 7(11,7,11)sts and place them on a safety pin, CHANGE TO LARGER NEEDLES, and work across rem. 48(48,64,64)sts as for row 1 of lace pattern.

Work straight in pattern until front is one complete pattern shorter than the back, so ending with a 16th row and at the neck edge. (The same edge as the sts left on a safety pin.)

Shape neck:

Next row – Pattern 14sts, place them on a holder, pattern to end.

Next row – Pattern to last 2sts, work 2 tog.

**Cont. in pattern, dec. 1st. at neck edge only on next row also, then cont. in pattern on rem. 32(32,48,48)sts until the last pattern rep. is completed so that the front matches the back to the shoulder.

Cast off.

Right Front

With 3¼mm needles, cast on 51(55,67,71)sts and work 4 rows of rib in the same way as given for the back.

Next row – Making a buttonhole, rib 2(4,2,4), cast off 3, rib to end.

Next row – Rib, casting on 3 over the 3 cast off on the previous row.

Cont. in rib until work measures 5cm ending with row 1, and inc. by 4sts evenly over the last row. (55,59,71,75sts)

Next row – Change to 4mm needles and work:

Work as given for row 1 of pattern as far as last 7(11,7,11)sts, turn, leaving these sts on a safety pin and cont. on rem. 48(48,64,64)sts in lace pattern.

Work straight in pattern until front is one complete pattern shorter than the back, so ending with a 16th row and at the armhole edge. (The opposite edge to the sts left on the safety pin.)

Shape Neck:

Next row – Pattern until 14sts rem., turn, placing these 14sts on a holder, work 2tog, pattern to end.

Work as for left front from ** to end.

Sleeves

With 3¼mm needles, cast on 43(45,47,47)sts and work 5cm in
    rib in the same way as given for the back, ending with row 1
    and inc. evenly across this last row by 7(5,3,3)sts.
    (50,50,50,50sts)
Change to 4mm needles and work the next row:
P1,K16,P16,K16,P1.
Using this as a foundation row, from now on work the centre
    panel of 16sts in st.st., and the two outer panels of 16sts in
    the lace pattern, cont. with the next row as 2nd row of the
    pattern and all inc. which follow will be added to the outer
    edges in plain st.st. The next row will therefore be worked
    in K.
Cont. to work the two pattern panels as set, the centre panel in
    st.st., and adding all inc. in plain st.st. to the sides, inc. 1st
    at each end of the next, then every foll. 5th(4th,3rd,3rd)row
    until there are 94(104,110,116)sts.
Work straight to a total measurement of approximately
    43(44,44,46)cm ending after a complete pattern rep.
Cast off loosely.

Button Band

With 3¼mm needles and with right side facing, work the
    7(11,7,11)sts from the safety pin at the left front welt as for
    row 1 of rib as given for the back.
Cont. in rib as before, until band, when slightly stretched,
    reaches as far as the top of the front neck edge.
Leave sts on a holder, breaking off yarn.
Mark a point on the button band 8cm below the top, and a point
    to match the buttonhole on the right front welt.
Evenly space and mark 4 further points between these two.

Buttonhole Band

Work as given for button band, but from the sts on a pin at the
    right front welt, working a buttonhole as before to match
    each marked point and ending with a row 2, i.e. at the
    outside edge.
Do not break off yarn.

Neckband

Join both shoulder seams matching pattern. With 3¼mm needles
and with right side facing, rib across the sts at the top of the
buttonhole band, then pick up and K the 14sts from the
holder at the right front neck, 18sts up the right neck slope,
the 32(48,32,48) sts from the back neck holder, dec. by 1st
in the middle, 18sts down the left neck slope, and the 14sts
from the left neck holder, rib the sts from the top of the
button band. (109,133,109,133sts)
Starting with row 2,rib 3 rows.
Rib 2 more rows, working a buttonhole as before at the right
front neck.
Rib 3 further rows.
Cast off in rib.

To Make Up

Do not press.
Join rem. seams matching pattern, and ensuring that armholes
are 22(24,25,27)cm deep after making up. Stitch on buttons
to match button holes.

A Knitting Widower's Lament

This never ending clicking
Makes me shout and blubber.
Why doesn't somebody invent
Knitting pins made of rubber.

CONTRIBUTED BY
CATHERINE FLETCHER

9 Aran Diagonal Jumper

Aran knitting

Many people are put off Aran knitting by the apparent
complexity of the patterns. If you have never tried a cable and
texture like this, do have a go. It isn't difficult, it's just rather
slow until you get going. Once you have knitted a few rows you
will begin to see how the pattern is formed and it soon becomes
second nature.

If you keep losing your way in the pattern fasten a hair grip
or a paper clip to the edge of the page, alongside the appropriate
line of text, and keep moving it down as you work each row. You
can even buy gadgets now that will do this for you.

One of the most useful things I find with Aran knitting is a
cranked cable needle. These are ordinary cable needles, except
that they have a bend in the middle, which prevents them from
falling out of the stitches at the back of your work. They really
are very helpful.

It will also help you to remember where you are if you mark
the rows in regular groups, for instance mark every tenth row, or
the last row in each pattern repeat, or the rows on which you
cable. I find this last idea especially helpful, as it is often difficult
to decide which was the last row on which the cabling was done.

How do you mark your rows? There are several ways.
Simply thread a short length of contrast yarn through the last
stitch, or thread in a paper clip, or a safety pin, or even the
special little split rings in different colours and sizes which are
designed for the job.

This striking modern diagonal Aran jumper, designed by
Jennie Watson, was a runner up in the ORACLE knitting Design
competition, and was knitted in a rich salmon pink.

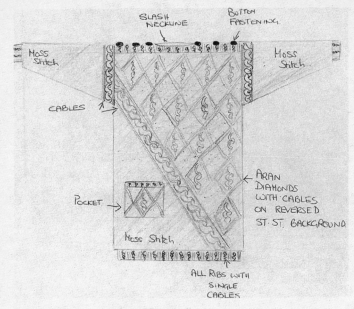

Aran Diagonal Jumper, original design by Jennie Watson.

Aran Diagonal Jumper

Materials

Spectrum Aran in:
Nasturtium Orange: 9(10) × 100g balls

1 pr. 5mm (No. 6) needles, 1 pr. 4½mm (No. 7) needles and 1 pr. 4mm (No. 8) needles.

1 cable needle and 6 buttons.

Measurements

To fit:	up to	38	up to	44in
		97		112cm
Actual measurement:		40		46in
		102		117cm

Length (approx):	30	30in
	76	76cm
Underarm seam:	18	18in
	46	46cm

Tension

18sts and 24 rows = 10cm (4in) on 5mm (No. 6) needles over st.st.

Special Abbreviations

C3B (Cross 3 back) = slip next st. on to a cable needle and hold at back of work, K next 2sts from left-hand needle, then K st. from cable needle.

C3F (Cross 3 front) = slip next 2sts on to a cable needle and hold at front of work, K next st. from left-hand needle, then K sts from cable needle.

C4B (Cable 4 back) = slip next 2sts on to a cable needle and hold at back of work, K the next 2sts from left-hand needle then K sts from cable needle.

C8B (Cable 8 back) = slip next 4sts on to a cable needle and hold at back of work, K next 4sts from left-hand needle then K sts from cable needle.

T3B (Twist 3 back) = slip next st. on to a cable needle and hold at back of work, K the next 2sts from left-hand needle, then P st. from cable needle.

T3F (Twist 3 front) = slip next 2sts on to a cable needle and hold at front of work, P next st. from left-hand needle then K sts from cable needle.

Diamond Aran Pattern

Worked over 16sts on a background of rev. st.st.
First row – Right side. P6,C4B,P6.
2nd row – K6,P4,K6.
3rd row – P5,C3B,C3F,P5.
4th row – K5,P6,K5.
5th row – P4,C3B,K2,C3F,P4.
6th row – K4,P8,K4.
7th row – P3,T3B,C4B,T3F,P3.
8th row – K3,P2,K1,P4,K1,P2,K3.
9th row – P2,T3B,P1,K4,P1,T3F,P2.
10th row – K2,P2,K2,P4,K2,P2,K2.

11th row – P1,T3B,P2,C4B,P2,T3F,P1.
12th row – K1,P2,K3,P4,K3,P2,K1.
13th row – T3B,P3,K4,P3,T3F.
14th row – P2,K4,P4,K4,P2.
15th row – K2,P4,C4B,P4,K2.
16th row – As 14th row.
17th row – T3F,P3,K4,P3,T3B.
18th row – As 12th row.
19th row – P1,T3F,P2,C4B,P2,T3B,P1.
20th row – As 10th row.
21st row – P2,T3F,P1,K4,P1,T3B,P2.
22nd row – As 8th row.
23rd row – P3,T3F,C4B,T3B,P3.
24th row – As 6th row.
25th row – P4,T3F,K2,T3B,P4.
26th row – As 4th row.
27th row – P5,T3F,T3B,P5.
28th row – As 2nd row.

Front

Using 4mm needles, cast on 114(124)sts and work:
Row 1 – K1, *K2,P2,K4,P2*, rep. from * to * to last 3 sts, K3.
Row 2 and every alt. row – K1,P2, *K2,P4,K2,P2*, rep. from * to * to last st.,K1.
Row 3 – K1,*K2,P2,C4B,P2*, rep. from * to * to last 3sts, K3.
Row 5 – As row 1.
Row 6 – As row 2.
Rep. these 6 rows twice more, inc. by 6sts evenly across the final row on the larger size only. (114,130)sts**
Change to 5mm needles and work the next row:
K1, *P6,C4B,P6*, rep. from * to * once(twice) more, P to last st., K1.
Using this as the foundation row, (first row) of the Diamond Aran Pattern, work the next 27 rows of the pattern forming these 2(3) diamonds only, with the 2 edge sts in K and the remainder of the work in rev. st.st.
Next row – K1, *P6,C4B,P6*, rep. from * to * twice(3 times) more, P to last st., K1.
Work the further 27 rows of the pattern, forming these 3(4) diamonds only on the background as before.
****Cont. in this way, with the 2 edge sts always in K, the

background in rev. st.st. throughout, and adding an extra
diamond pattern rep. to the inside edge of the patterned area
on each first row of the pattern, until there are 7(8) diamonds
across the work, occupying the whole width, and the 28
pattern rows have been worked 6 times in all. AT THE SAME
TIME, when there are 5(6) complete diamond patterns across
the work, and the 28 pattern rows have been worked 4 times,
cont. to keep pattern correct, shape underarms:

Cast on 18sts at beg. of next row and work these sts:
K3,P2,K8,P2,K3, pattern to end of row.

Cast on 18sts at beg. of next row and work these sts:
K1,P2,K2,P8,K2,P2,K1, pattern to last 18sts, rep. from * to
* . (150,166)sts

Cont. to keep central pattern correct and progressing as before,
work each group of 18sts at either side, at the same time, in
the foll. way:

Row 1 – K3,P2,K8,P2,K3.

Row 2 and every alt. row – K1,P2,K2,P8,K2,P2,K1.

Row 3 – As row 1.

Row 5 – K3,P2,C8B,P2,K3.

Row 7 – As row 1.

Row 8 – As row 2.

Rep. these 8 rows throughout remainder of work on the 18sts at
each side of the work to form sleeve head cable.

When the 28 row diamond aran pattern repeats have been
completed 6 times, cont. to keep pattern correct on the 18sts
at either side of the work, and remaining on main needles,
work the centre 114(130)sts:

Next row – K1(2),P2 on larger size only, *K2,P2,K4,P2*, rep.
from * to * to last 3(6)sts ,K2,P2 on larger size only, K1(2).

Using this as a foundation row, work 12 rows in all of cabled rib
in the same way as given for the welt, cabling each set of 4
right side sts on the 3rd, then the foll. 6th row as before.

Cast off.

Back

Work as given for front as far as **.

Change to 5mm needles and work the next row:

K1,P to last 33(49)sts, *P6,C4B,P6*, rep. from * to *
once(twice) more, K1.

Work as given for front from *** to ***.

Next row – K1,P to last 49(65) sts, *P6,C4B,P6*, rep. from * to
    * twice (three times) more, K1.
Work the further 27 rows of the pattern forming these 3(4)
    diamonds only on the background as before.
Work as for front from **** to end.
(This will give a back and front alike, except that the diagonal
    travels in the reverse direction.)

Sleeves (same for both sizes)

Using 4mm needles, cast on 44sts and work 18 rows of cabled rib
    in the same way as given for the front welt, inc. by 6sts
    evenly across the last row. (50sts)
Change to 5mm needles and rev. st.st. starting with a P row, and
    inc. 1st. at each end of the 2nd, then every foll. 4th row
    until there are 90sts.
Work straight to a total length of 41cm.
Cast off loosely.

Front diagonal cable

Using 5mm needles, cast on 2sts.
Row 1 – K1, inc. 1st. in last st. in K.
Row 2 – Inc. 1st. in first st. in P,P1,K1.
Cont. in this way, inc. at the left-hand edge of every row (i.e. the
    end of each right side row, and the beg. of each wrong side
    row), until there are 18sts. AT THE SAME TIME, working
    all increased sts into the 8-row pattern given for the sleeve
    head cable on the front and back.
When there are 18sts, cont. to keep pattern correct, rep. the 8
    pattern rows until cable, when slightly stretched, reaches
    across the work with its diagonal short beg. edge at the top
    of the bottom welt, and its long edge parallel with the
    pattern, so that the work is long enough to reach the side
    edge of the front.
Cont. to keep pattern correct, dec. 1st. at the same edge as the edge
    which was increased at the beg., on every row until 2sts rem.
Work 2 tog, fasten off.

Back diagonal cable

Work as given for front diagonal cable, but inc. and dec. to

58

shape the beg. and end at the opposite right-hand edge, so
that this cable will slope the other way to match the pattern
on the back.

Pocket

Using 5mm needles, cast on 34sts and work:
First row – K1, *P6,C4B,P6*, rep. from * to * once more, K1.
Using this as a foundation row, work the rem. 27 Diamond Aran
Pattern rows over these 2 patterns once.
Change to needles 1 size smaller, i.e. 4½mm and work 6 cable
rib rows in the same way as given for the front welt.
Cast off in rib.

To Make Up

Do not press.
Join shoulders by top edges of cable only, matching pattern. Join
all rem. seams matching patterns. Attach diagonal cables
evenly. Attach pocket centrally to the front rev. st.st. area.
Lap the front neck 2cm over the back neck at each shoulder
and stitch together by attaching 3 buttons at each shoulder,
evenly spaced, to give a central neck opening of 23cm.

This pattern is headed:
'READY FOR THE
TRENCHES. He's ready for
the firing line, proudly
displaying his shooting glove.
Remember, a brave man's
life may depend on the quick
obedience of his right hand.'

10 Cats Jumper

Picture knitting

Sometimes called 'Intarsia' knitting, this technique involves working blocks of different colours from a chart to create a pattern or a picture.

If you are unfamiliar with using charts, there are notes to guide you on page 61, and these will also help you with the charts in this particular book.

Because you are working in more than one colour on any row, you may be tempted to strand across the back with the colour or colours which you are not using. This gives a very thick bulky fabric, is slow to do, and spoils the knitting by pulling it in and so making the fabric lumpy and distorting the shape of the picture.

Instead of stranding colours across the back, work each block of stitches with a separate strand of yarn, then, at the end of the colour block, twist the old colour firmly once around the new and leave the old colour behind so that it is there ready on the way back on the next row.

This method gives a much more satisfying neat flat picture, but also brings two problems of its own. Firstly, you will have a length of yarn for every patch of colour, and so may get in a tangle. Don't leave each ball of yarn attached, or you may end up in a terrible tangle. Instead cut short lengths, just as much as you will need for the patch of colour, and either let them hang, sorting them out when they get muddled, or, if they are rather longer, wind them on to yarn bobbins, which you can either buy or make from card.

The second common problem with unstranded picture knitting is that knitters finish a garment and then have a depressingly large number of coloured ends hanging from the back of the knitting, which they then propose to sew in with a needle. Rather than leaving yourself with this laborious task, as you begin and end each colour patch, weave the loose end in at the back of the adjacent stitches and then it can be simply cut off. This technique gives just the same result as weaving in later with a sewing needle, and is so much quicker, as well as being done as you go along, rather than being left as a horrible job at the end.

Using charts, especially the ones in this book

Using charts for picture knitting is so much easier than having the colours written out for you stitch by stitch and row by row. This is mainly because you can actually see what you are going to knit, so that you can watch it grow like the picture on the chart, and allow one row to relate to the row before, instead of blindly following a list of numbers.

If you are working from a black-and-white chart, why not colour it in before you begin, or, better still, get the children to do it for you; it will make it much easier to follow.

There are several things which you can do to help you to keep your place on a chart. Some knitters number the rows as they go along, some cross them out. You could cover them with another sheet of paper, or mark them with a clip, or even use a specially designed gadget which you can buy from your wool shop.

Finally, do remember that the charts are a guide, not a rule book, if you would rather have black cats, or green trees, then you are the boss, and for things like abstracts, wavy lines and zigzags, you can really put them wherever you wish on the jumper.

A special note on the larger charts in this book
In order to enable us to keep the charts for the larger pictures in this book easier to use, we have 'cut them up' on to several pages, so do check carefully before you begin, comparing the charts with the garment in the photograph, and making sure that you begin in the right place. You could photocopy the charts and join them into one, but take care if you also enlarge them that they are all enlarged to the same scale so that they fit together correctly.

The charming cat picture jumper overleaf was a runner up in the ORACLE Knitting Design Competition, and was designed by Mrs M. Thomas.

Cats Jumper,
original design by
Mrs M. Thomas.

Cats Jumper

Materials

Spectrum Detroit Chunky in:
Royal: 5(5,6,6) × 100g balls
Plus Primrose Yellow, Black, Tangerine Orange, Baby Blue:
1 × 100g ball of each colour for all sizes.
Plus Spectrum Arizona Brushed Chunky in:
White: 1(1,1,1) × 100g ball

1 pr. 6mm (No. 4) needles, 1 pr. 5mm (No. 6) needles.

Using the picture charts for this pattern

To help you to use the charts for this jumper, there are some
notes on page 61.

Measurements

To fit:	34	36	38	40in
	86	91	97	102cm
Actual measurement:	38	40	42	44in
	97	102	107	112cm
Length (approx):	24	24	25	25in
	61	61	63	63cm
Underarm length:	17½	18	18	18in
	44	46	46	46cm

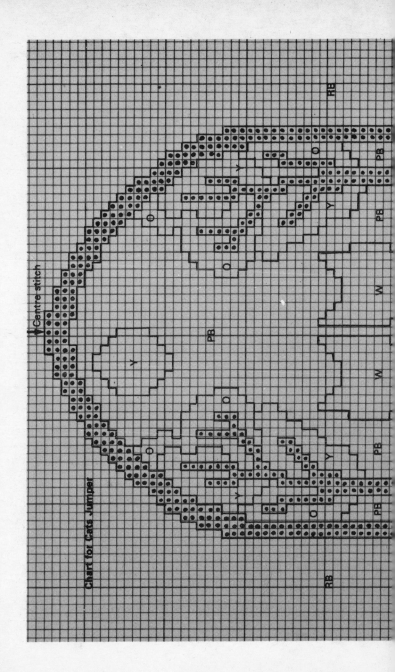

Chart for Cats Jumper

Centre stitch

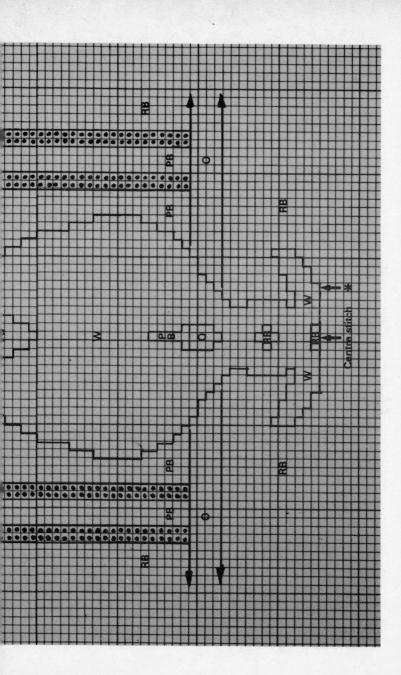

Key to Chart

● = black

All other colour blocks as marked:

Y = yellow

O = orange

PB = pale blue

RB = royal blue (main colour) (MC)

Arrowed st. marked * = 28th(30th,32nd,34th) st. of the 3rd(3rd,7th,7th) st.st. row.

Complete orange rows to edges of work.

Tension

14sts and 18 rows = 10cm (4in) on 6mm (No. 4) needles over st.st.

N.B. The jumper is worked in Main Colour (Royal Blue), with the cat picture on the front only. All other pieces in plain MC only.

Front

Using 5mm needles and MC, cast on 64(64,68,72)sts and work:

Row 1 – K1,(K2,P2) to last 3sts, K3.

Row 2 – K1,(P2,K2) to last 3sts, P2,K1.

Rep. these 2 rows until rib measures 5cm ending with row 2, and inc. by 3(7,7,7)sts evenly across the last row. 67(71,75,79)sts

Change to 6mm needles and st.st. starting with a K row.**

Work in plain MC to beg. of chart, then work the chart placing it as given.

When chart is complete, work 2 rows of MC.

Shape neck:

Next row – K28(30,31,33) turn, leaving rem.sts on a spare needle, P2 tog tbl,P to end.

***Working on these sts only, dec. 1st. at neck edge only on next 2 rows, then on every alt. row until 23(25,26,28)sts rem.

work 2 rows straight, so ending with a P row.

Cast off.***

Rejoin yarn to rem.sts at inside edge, K11(11,13,13) and place them on a holder, K to end.

Next row – P to last 2, P2 tog.
Rep. from *** to ***.

Back

Work as given for front as far as **.

Work straight in plain MC until back matches front to shoulder, ending with a P row.

Next row – Cast off 23(25,26,28)sts, K until 23(25,26,28)sts remain, place the 21(21,23,23)sts just worked on to a holder, cast off to end.

Sleeves

Using 5mm needles and MC, cast on 28(28,32,32)sts and work 5cm in rib in the same way as given for the front, ending with row 2.

Change to 6mm needles and st.st. starting with a K row, and inc. 1 st. at each end of every foll. 3rd row until there are 64(66,68,70)sts.

Work straight to a total length of 44(46,46,46) cm ending with a P row.

Cast off.

Neckband

Join left shoulder seam.

Using 5mm needles and MC, with right side facing, pick up and K the 21(21,23,23)sts from the back neck holder, 12sts down the left neck slope, the 11(11,13,13)sts from the front neck holder, and 12sts up the right neck slope. 56(56,60,60sts).

Starting with row 2, work 6 rows of rib in the same way as before.

Cast off very loosely in rib.

To Make Up

Do not press.

Join rem. seams ensuring that armholes are 23(24,24,25) cm deep after making up. The white of the cats may be carefully brushed.

11 Jade Dragon

Adding surface decoration

There are lots of ways in which you can decorate knitting after it is completed, perhaps because you would like to be particularly creative with a design which lends itself to surface textures, or perhaps because you are a novice knitter and would like to create a complex jumper for which you have not yet learnt the advanced knitting skills.

For either reason, or perhaps for both, you can have tremendous fun with surface decoration of knitting. Think of the possibilities of fabric or knitted appliqué, sequins, embroidery, plaits, tassels, ribbons, couched yarns and threads, decorative buttons, pockets and patches. More exotically, add detachable puppets, toys and creatures, fabric paints, badges and motifs, and even glass and pottery.

Whatever you would like to add to your knitting there are several things which need to be taken into consideration, some obvious, some less so.

Most importantly, especially for children's garments, are the trims and decorations safe? Embroidery is probably safest. Any other trims must be very firmly stitched on, be non toxic, and not sharp in any way, as their small wearers will probably try to eat them. Think especially about ribbon. It is very tempting to thread it around the necks of jumpers, but it must be firmly stitched in at least two places or it becomes a potential noose.

It is worth considering too whether or not the additional materials will wash because, if not, then you will have the tedious job of removing and replacing them each time you launder the garment. Fabrics like felt don't wash, and look out for dyes which run. If in doubt you could always experiment on tension squares.

Jade Dragon, original design by Andrea Fish.

Sequins should wash with care but check the manufacturers' instructions first. If you are appalled at the thought of sewing on thousands of sequins, or beads, you can now buy beautiful motifs already made which are simply tacked on like badges.

Be sure also that the additions that you make are not too heavy. Some beads and buttons are very large, and I have seen jumpers over-decorated with bits of pierced pottery and stained glass. An excess of this kind of decoration is clearly going to be too much of a good thing, as the garment will be heavy and difficult to wear, and the weight will, sooner or later, distort the knitting.

One of the best things to decorate knitting with is knitting. Try patches and shapes, frills and picot edges, pennants and points, bumps and bobbles, all of which are easily knitted.

This beautiful jade dragon is an ideal jumper on which to give your imagination free rein. Ours is decorated with embroidery, knitted bobbles, sequin strips and gilt studs, and was a runner up in the ORACLE Knitting Design competition. The jumper was designed by Andrea Fish.

Jade Dragon

Materials

Spectrum Detroit Double Knit in:
Main Colour, Opal Green: 4(4,5) × 100g balls
Contrast, Serpentine Jade: 1(1,1) × 100g ball

1 frog fastening or similar, and yarn scraps and trims for decoration.

1 pr. 4mm (No. 8) needles, 1 pr. 3¾mm (No .9) and 1 pr. 3¼mm (No. 10) needles.

Using the picture charts for this pattern

To help you to use the charts for this jumper, there are some notes on page 61.

Measurements

To fit:	32–34	36–38	40– 42in
	81–86	91–97	102–107cm
Actual measurement:	38	42	46in
	97	107	117cm
Length:	26	26	26in
	66	66	66cm
Underarm length:	18	18	18in
	46	46	46cm

Tension

22sts and 30 rows = 10cm (4in) on 4mm (No. 8) needles over st.st.

Key to Chart

Dragon motif completely in pale jade
All rem. background dark jade green

○ = make bobble in this st. i.e. work 3 times into this st., turn and work 3, turn and work 3, turn and work 3, turn and work 3 tog. (St.st. bobble to appear on the right side.)

71

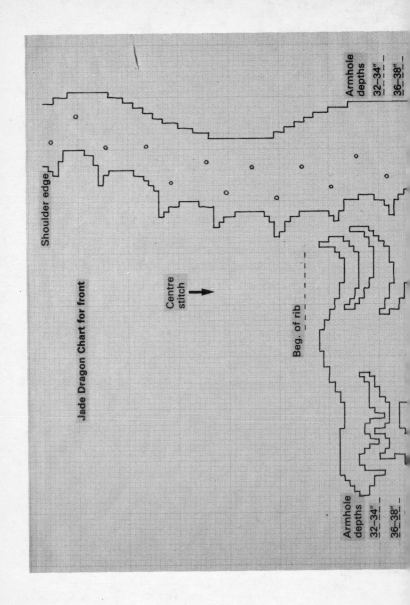

Jade Dragon Chart for front

Shoulder edge

Centre stitch →

Beg. of rib

Armhole
depths
32–34" __
__ __
36–38" __

Armhole
depths
32–34" __
__ __
36–38" __

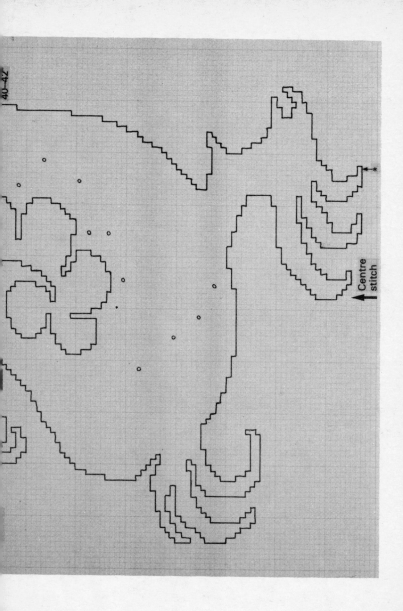

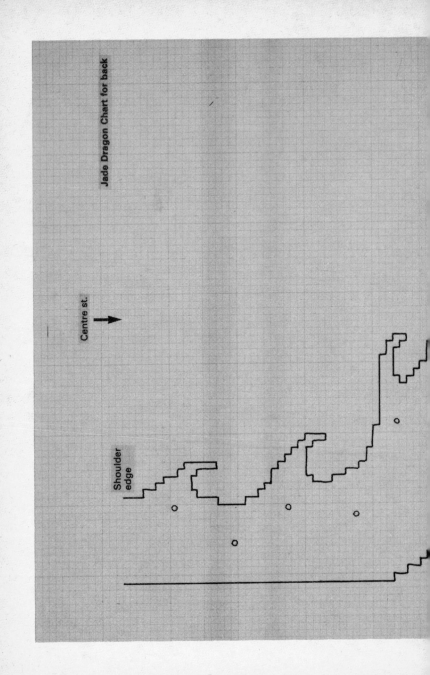

Jade Dragon Chart for back

Centre st. →

Shoulder edge

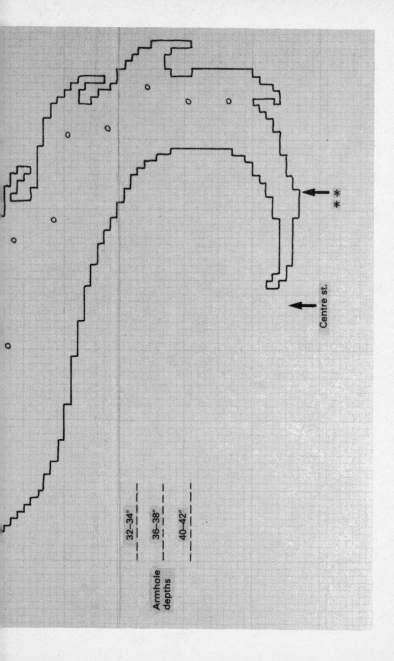

Armhole
depths

32–34"

36–38"

40–42"

Centre st.

**

Arrowed st. marked * on chart for front is 28th(33rd,39th) st. of 39th st.st. row, i.e. 39th row after the 2½cm welt rib.

Arrowed st. marked ** on chart for back is 37th(42nd,48th) st. of 97th st.st. row after the welt, i.e. this chart begins when work is 58 rows longer than at the beginning of the chart for the front.

Front

Using 3¾mm needles, cast on 105(115,127)sts and work:
Row 1 – K1,(K1,P1) to last 2sts, K2.
Row 2 – K1,(P1,K1) to end.
Rep. these 2 rows until rib measures 2½cm ending with row 2.
Change to 4mm needles and work next row, keeping rib correct, rib 7, K to last 7sts, rib 7.
Next row – Rib 7, P to last 7sts, rib 7.
Rep. these 2 rows until work measures 10cm ending with a P row.
Change to plain st.st. starting with a K row and, omitting ribbed edges from now on, work straight to a total length, as shown on chart for front, of 43(42,41) cm ending with a P row, AT THE SAME TIME commencing the chart, placing it as shown.

Shape armholes
Cont. to keep chart correct throughout remainder of work.
Cast off 8sts at beg. of next 2 rows. 89(99,111)sts.**
Work straight until armholes measure 5(6,8) cm ending with a P row, as shown on the chart.

Beg. neck rib
Cont. to keep chart correct.
Next row – K37(42,48), (K1,P1) 7 times, K1,K rem. 37(42,48)sts.
Next row – P37(42,48), K1,(K1,P1) 6 times, K2,P rem. 37(42,48)sts.
Rep. these 2 rows 3 more times (8 rows in all), so working a 15st. band up the centre, of which the centre 13sts are rib and the outer 2sts are always in K.

Divide for neck
K37(42,48), (K1,P1) 3 times, inc. 1st. in next st. in K, turn, leaving rem.sts on a holder, K1,(P1,K1) 3 times, K1,P to end. 45(50,56)sts.

Working on this side only:

Next row – K37(42,48), (K1,P1) 3 times, K2.

Next row – K1,(P1,K1) 3 times, K1,P to end.

***Rep. these 2 rows until armhole measures 15(17,18) cm ending at neck edge, and when 22 rows of chart rem. to be worked:

Shape neck

Rib 8sts as before and place them on a safety pin, work to end.

Dec 1st. at neck edge only on next 5 rows, then on every alt. row until 28(33,39)sts rem.

Work 8 rows straight, so ending with a P row, and completing the chart.

Cast off.***

Rejoin yarn to inside edge of rem.sts and work:

Next row – K2(P1,K1) 3 times, K to end.

Next row – P37(42,48), K1,(K1,P1) 3 times, K1.

Work as for other side of neck from *** to ***, noting that the chart does not apply.

Back

Work as given for front as far as ** but working from chart for back.

Work straight, working from chart for back, until back matches front to shoulder so ending with a P row and completing the chart.

Next row – Working sts in the same colours as on the previous row, cast off 28(33,39), K until 28(33,39)sts rem., place the 33sts just worked on a holder, cast off to end.

Sleeves

Using 3¼mm needles, cast on 45(49,51)sts and work 2½cm of rib in the same way as given for the front, ending with row 2.

Change to 4mm needles, and work:

Next row – K16(18,19), (K1,P1) 6 times, K1,K rem. 16(18,19)sts.

Next row – P16(18,19), K1,(K1,P1) 5 times, K2, P rem. 16(18,19)sts.

Rib the centre 13sts in this way until work measures 10cm, keeping all rem. sts in st.st., then change to st.st. across the whole of the sleeve throughout the remainder of the work,

AT THE SAME TIME inc. 1st. at each end of the 3rd, then
every foll. 4th row until there are 99(105,111)sts.

Work straight to a total length of 46cm ending with a K row and
mark both ends of this row.

Work 11 further rows, so ending with a P row.

Cast off loosely .

Neckband (same for all sizes)

Join both shoulder seams, matching picture.

Using 3¼mm needles, and with right side facing, pick up and
rib the 8sts from the pin at the right front neck, pick up and
K20sts up the right neck slope, the 33sts from the back
neckholder, 20sts down the left neck slope, and rib the 8sts
from the pin at the left front neck. (89sts)

Starting with row 2, rib 8 rows in the same way as given for the
front welt.

Cast off in rib.

To Make Up

Do not press.

Join rem. seams, noting that the bottom 8cm of each side seam is
left open, and that the marked point on the sleeves is the
underarm, with the remainder of the sleeve head matching
the armhole with the corners also matching.

Attach chosen fastening at neck. Decorate the dragon with
contrast embroidery and chosen trims.

There was a young lady from Bude
Who purled and who plained in the nude.
She knitted a sweater
To cover her better,
T'was warmer and not quite so rude.

CONTRIBUTED BY MRS HAGGER

12 Shelby's Desert Jacket

Jackets and coats

Knitted jackets and coats can look very spectacular, and although they involve a great deal of work, it is definitely worth it in the end.

Before you begin, make sure that the size, and especially the length, is going to both fit and suit you. It is especially important not to knit a coat or jacket too long, as it will tend to drop anyway, and you could end up looking like Dopey in *Snow White and the Seven Dwarves*. If you have set your heart on a pattern that is too long, then adapt it carefully before you start, as, often, shortening a pattern is the easiest alteration to make. Simply don't knit as much.

If a piece of knitting is especially large, perhaps a coat made in one piece, then do consider working on circular needles. They are not only useful for knitting in the round, but are very good at accommodating large numbers of stitches, and you can simply work back and forth on them as you would on a pair of needles.

Some people hate using circular needles. If you do, another possibility is to work across a series of double-ended needles, using them in sequence and then working back, rather than in the round. You will tend, however, to lose stitches from the needles, and you may have to use stitch stoppers. A circular needle is much easier if you could bear to persevere.

Since a coat or jacket can be such a labour of love, as well as being potentially expensive, it may be worth considering lining it. Especially if it is rather long, this will help to prevent it from 'seating' and from developing bumps at the elbows.

This gorgeous Desert Scene Jacket was designed by Shelby Pizzarro-Longbottom, and was the over-all winner in the ORACLE Knitting Design Competition.

Shelby's Desert Jacket, winning design by Shelby Pizzarro-Longbottom.

Shelby's Desert Jacket

Materials

Spectrum Detroit Double Knit in:
Dark Brown (Brown): 1(1) × 100g ball
Brown (Cognac): 1(1) × 100g ball
Orange (Tangerine): 1(1) × 100g ball
Yellow (Primrose): 1(2) × 100g ball
Pink (Pink): 1(1) × 100g ball
Lilac (Plumage): 1(1) × 100g ball
Pale Blue (Baby Blue): 1(1) × 100g ball
Royal Blue (Royal): 2(2) × 100g balls
White (White): 1(1) × 100g ball

Scrap of black for embroidery.

12 buttons

1 pr. 4mm (No. 8) needles, 1 pr. 3¼mm (No. 10) needles.

81

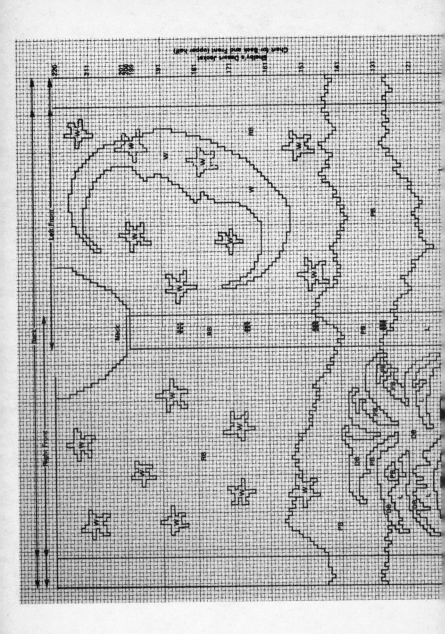

Chart for Back and Front (upper half)
Bradley's Deluxe Jacket

82

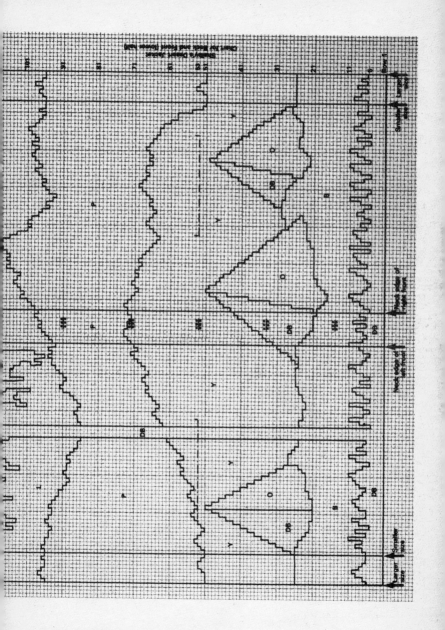

Using the picture charts for this pattern

To help you to use the charts for this jumper, there are some notes on page 61.

Measurements

To fit:	up to	36	up to	42in
		91		107cm
Actual measurement:		44		50in
		112		127cm
Length:		30		30in
		76		76cm
Underarm length:		17		17in
		43		43cm

Tension

22sts and 30 rows = 10cm (4in) on 4mm (No. 8) needles over st.st.

Key to Chart

Colour blocks as marked.
N.B. Moon on left front only.

— — — — = Stars which replace moon on back only.

—.—.— = Pocket position.

Dark brown (DB) = Brown
Brown (B) = Cognac
Orange (O) = Tangerine
Yellow (Y) = Primrose
Pink (P) = Pink
Lilac (L) = Plumage
Pale Blue (PB) = Baby Blue
Royal Blue (RB) = Royal Blue
White (W) = White

Back

Using dark brown and main-sized needles, i.e. 4mm, cast on
121(137)sts and work:
Row 1 – K1,(K1,P1) to last 2sts, K2.
Row 2 – K1,(P1,K1) to end.
Rep. these 2 rows twice more. (6 rib rows in all)
Change to st.st. starting with a K row and commence chart, with
this first st.st. row as row 1.
Work the complete chart for the back, omitting the front division
and the moon, but adding the optional stars.
When the last P row of the chart is complete, work the next row
in plain royal blue:
Cast off 43(51)sts, K until 43(51)sts rem., place the 35(35)sts just
worked on to a holder, cast off to end.

Pocket Linings (make 2)

Using 4mm needles and yellow, cast on 27sts and work 51 rows
in st.st. starting and ending with a K row.
Leave sts on a spare needle.

Left Front

Using 4mm needles and dark brown, cast on 65(73)sts and work
6 rib rows in the same way as for the back.
Next row – Work from the chart, working only those sts for the
left front, working in st.st., starting with a K row, but
keeping the 7sts at the opening neck edge always in rib as
set, working these sts also in the colours given on the chart.
Work from the chart until 52 rows of st.st. and chart have been
worked, then work the next row, placing the pocket:
**Cont. to keep the chart correct, K36(44)sts, place the last 27sts
just worked on to a holder, K to last 7sts, rib to end.
Next row – Cont. to keep rib, st.st. and chart correct, work as far
as the sts left on the holder, then place the pocket lining
with its st.st. side facing the main piece and pattern across
the sts from the pocket lining, pattern to end.
Cont. to work from the chart, keeping pattern and colour correct
until neck shaping is reached, so ending with row 199, a K
row.

***Shape neck*: (cont. to keep chart correct)

Next row – Rib and pattern 10sts, place them on a safety pin, work 2 tog, pattern to end.

Dec. 1st. at neck edge only on next 6 rows, then on next 5 alt. rows. 43(51)sts rem.

Work 4 rows straight so ending with a P row and with last row of chart.

Cast off.

Right Front

Work as given for left front BUT work from the chart for the right front, and reverse all shapings and work buttonholes, as follows:

Work buttonholes – In the 3rd rib row, rib 2, cast off 3, rib to end.

Next row, rib, casting on 3 over the 3 cast off on the previous row.

The 7 rib sts will be up the right-hand edge.

When working the chart, work the buttonholes as marked in the 7 rib sts in the same way as before.

Work from the chart for the right front until 52 rows of st.st. and chart have been completed, then work the next row, placing the pocket, not as given at ** but reversing the shaping:

Cont. to keep chart correct, rib 7, K49(49) place the last 27sts just worked on to a holder, K to end.

Place pocket lining on the next row in the same way as for the right front.

Cont. straight from the chart, keeping pattern, rib, buttonholes and st.st. correct until neck shaping is reached, so ending with row 200, a P row, then work as for left front from *** to end, noting that 1 less straight row will be needed to complete the chart.

Sleeves (both alike, and the same for both sizes)

Using 3¼mm needles and yellow, cast on 49sts and work 10 rows in rib as given for the back.

Change to 4mm needles and st.st. and work from the chart for the sleeve, inc. 1st. at each end of the 3rd, then every foll. 4th row until there are 99sts, then every foll. 3rd row until there are 111sts.

Work 1 row without shaping, the last row of the chart.

Cast off.

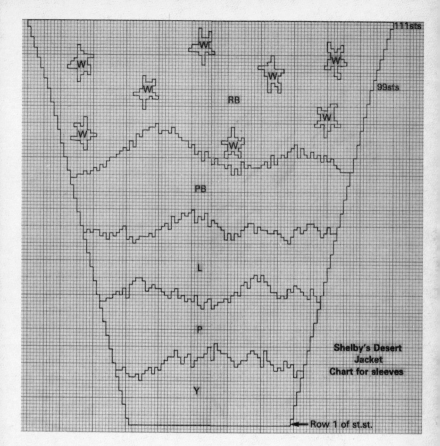

Shelby's Desert
Jacket
Chart for sleeves

← Row 1 of st.st.

Neckband

Join both shoulder seams. Using 3¼mm needles and royal blue,
   with right side facing and commencing at right neck front,
   pick up and rib the first 7sts from the safety pin, K the rem.
   3sts from the safety pin, pick up and K 24sts up the right
   front slope, the 35sts from the back neck holder, 24sts down
   the left front slope and the first 3sts from the second safety
   pin, rib the rem. 7sts from the safety pin. (103sts)
Starting with row 2, work 8 rib rows in the same way as before,
   working a buttonhole at the right front neck in the same way
   as before on the 4th and 5th rows.
Cast off in rib.

Pocket Tops

Using 4mm needles and with right side facing, and following the
colours on the chart, pick up the 27sts from the holder for
the pocket top and work them as row 1 of rib as given for
the back.
Work 5 further rib rows in the colours as given on the chart.
Cast off in self colour in rib.

To Make Up

Do not press.
Join rem. seams matching colours. Insert sleeves so that
armholes are approx. 25cm deep after making up, i.e. the
royal blue matches. Catch down the pocket linings and ribs.
Embroider in black the features on the moon. Stitch on
buttons to match buttonholes.